HOPING FOR PEACE IN THE
MIDDLE EAST

Divided by conflict, wishing for peace

Angela Royston

raintree

a Capstone company — publishers for children

Raintree is an imprint of Capstone Global Library
Limited, a company incorporated in England and
Wales having its registered office
at 264 Banbury Road, Oxford OX2 7DY
– Registered company number: 6695582

www.raintree.co.uk
myorders@raintree.co.uk

Text © Capstone Global Library Limited 2017
The moral rights of the proprietor have been
asserted.

Produced for Raintree by Calcium
Edited by Sarah Eason and John Andrews
Designed by Paul Myerscough
Picture research by Rachel Blount
Production by Victoria Fitzgerald
Originated by Capstone Global Library Ltd © 2017
Printed and bound in India

ISBN 978 1 4747 3119 5 (hardback)
20 19 18 17 16
10 9 8 7 6 5 4 3 2 1

ISBN 978 1 4747 3197 3 (paperback)
21 20 19 18 17
10 9 8 7 6 5 4 3 2 1

British Library Cataloguing in
Publication Data
A full catalogue record for this book is available
from the British Library

Acknowledgements
We would like to thank the following for permission
to reproduce photographs: iStockphoto: Ariel Dunn,
1r, Eric Delmar, 41t, Joel Carillet, 22b, 22bg, 26b,
28b, 32b, 35m, 36b, 38t, 41b, 44b, Juanmonio, 18br,
lawcain, 23t, Marie_Liss, 24b, rrodickbeiler, 18-19t,
19bg, 26t, 26bg, 27tr, 29t, 31t, 31bg, 39m, 39bg,
Suzi McGregor, 11; Shutterstock: Arkady Mazor, 9t,
Bukhavets Mikhail, throughout, ChameleonsEye,
19b, Dimitry Pistov, 34t, 34bg, Flavia Morlachetti,
1t, Ilya Andriyanov, throughout, Konstantnin, 8b,
Kryvan, 13t, Lisa F. Young, 1ml, mangojuicy, 10,
11bg, mikhail, 4t, Mikhail Levit, 38b, R. Gino Santa
Maria, throughout, Ryan Rodrick Beiler, 3b, 6t, 12b,
14b, 14bg, 15t, 16b, 17t, 20b, 21t, 25t, 30b, 45t,
Sadik Gulec, 7, Sergey Lavrentev, throughout, SJ
Travel Photo and Video, 1m, Tom Asz, throughout,
Zvonimir Atletic, 4b, 4bg; Wahat al-Salam - Neve
Shalom, 42b, 42bg, 43t; Wikimedia: Daniel
Bara'nek, 5b, Tom Spender, 37t, PikiWiki – Israel
Free Image Collection, 6b, 6bg.

Cover art reproduced with permission of:
iStockphoto: Ariel Dunn, bmr, Shutterstock:
Bodrumsurf, br, Bohdanov Bohdan, bl, Flavia
Morlachetti, t, Kavram, bbg, Ryan Rodrick
Beiler, tbg, SJ Travel Photo and Video, m,
Lisa F. Young, bml.

CONTENTS

THE LONGEST-RUNNING CONFLICT

The Middle East stretches along the southern and eastern shores of the Mediterranean Sea. Most Israelis follow the Jewish religion, while most Palestinians are Muslim, following the religion of Islam.

Israel and Palestine together cover about 26,000 square kilometres (10,000 square miles), an area less than the size of Belgium. Israelis and Palestinians have been in conflict over this land for more than 60 years.

The Dome of the Rock is a Muslim shrine in the centre of Old Jerusalem. It is built on Temple Mount, a site that is also sacred to Jews and Christians.

What is so special?

The lands of Israel and Palestine are important to three religions: Judaism, Christianity and Islam. The ancient city of Jerusalem is holy to Jews, Christians and Muslims. According to the **Hebrew** Bible, Israel is the homeland of the Jews.

During the late 19th and early 20th centuries, many Jews returned to the land known as Palestine. Jewish people had never stopped regarding this land as home.

In 1947, the **United Nations** voted to divide Palestine between Jews and Palestinians, who were already living there at the time.

Peace Pen Pals

This book looks at the struggles between Israel and Palestine through the eyes of two children on either side of the conflict. Through their letters to each other, we can learn more about what it is like to live through this endless clash of Middle Eastern peoples.

Thousands of Jews came to Jerusalem to escape attacks in the countries where they were born.

THE 1948 WAR

The United Nations vote divided Israel-Palestine equally between Jews and Palestinians, although at the time there were about 1.35 million Palestinian Arabs and 650,000 Jews. The Jewish people declared the birth of their new country, Israel, but the Palestinians rejected the division. In 1948, war broke out.

CHAPTER ONE

FIGHTING FOR LAND

In 1948, three Arab countries, Syria, Jordan and Egypt, joined the Palestinians in war against the Israeli Army but were defeated. By the end of the war, Israel had taken over almost 80 per cent of the former country of Palestine, between the River Jordan and the Mediterranean Sea.

Many Jews who came to Israel lived in communities called kibbutzim, where they lived and worked together.

The West Bank and the Gaza Strip
The remaining land that made up Palestine was taken over by Jordan and Egypt. The land occupied by Jordan became known as the West Bank, and that which was occupied by Egypt became known as the Gaza Strip.

Legacy of the Holocaust

Following the Holocaust of World War II (1939–1945), Israeli Jews were joined by Jews from Europe. The Holocaust is the name given to the persecution and murder of 6 million European Jews in German **Nazi** death camps during World War II. The Jewish **refugees** wanted to help to build a strong country where they could feel safe. This country was Israel.

This Palestinian child grew up in a refugee camp in the nearby country of Lebanon.

RIGHT OF RETURN

One of the big issues dividing Israelis and Palestinians today is whether Palestinian refugees have the right to return to their homes in Israel. The number of Palestinian refugees has hugely increased. There are now about 5 million Palestinian refugees, made up mostly of the original families and their descendants.

WRITE TO ME!

Jerusalem, Israel
January 2013
Dear Salma,
   You must be wondering why a Jewish boy in Jerusalem is writing to you, a Muslim girl in Ramallah. The reason is that I want to find out what life is like for Palestinians living in the West Bank.

I live in a suburb on the edge of Jerusalem. There are lots of trees and parks here.

Ramallah is 14 kilometres (9 miles) north of Jerusalem, but it is completely cut off from Jerusalem. Israelis cannot visit Ramallah. The Israeli government does not allow it and it would not be safe. Most people in Israel are Jewish, but many Palestinian Arabs live there, too. Most Palestinians are Muslims, but about 2 per cent are Christians.

יום פתיחת הדאר במחנה העולים ביח'ליד. כ'ו טבת חשי"א, 4.1.1951
Post office opening day Immigrants Camp Beit-Lid, 4.1.1951

My grandfather was taught in an outdoor school on a kibbutz.

WAR

We live only a few kilometres apart, but we never meet. We both go to school, and we both have families and friends. Are our lives really so very different? I wish our people weren't in conflict. Why can't we live together in peace?

I live with my family in an old house, on the outskirts of Jerusalem. I am 12 years old, and I have an older brother and sister. My grandfather came to Israel from Poland after most of his family were killed in the Holocaust (He was lucky to escape.) He says that when he arrived, he lived on a kibbutz. My grandmother came from England in the 1950s, and I have lots of cousins on her side of the family.

Will you write to me and tell me what your life is like?

Jacob

9

Israel captured the Sinai Desert but returned it to Egypt after 1979, when Egypt agreed not to attack Israel again.

Fighting over borders

Trouble continued after the 1948 ceasefire. Arab countries wanted to reclaim the land from the Israelis, and both sides bought weapons and fighter planes. In 1967, the Arab countries that bordered Israel-Palestine threatened to attack Israel. But on 5 June, Israel took action first and attacked Egypt.

In just six days, Israel defeated the Arab armies in what became known as the Six Day War. Israeli soldiers occupied the West Bank, taking the Sinai Desert from Egypt and the Golan Heights from Syria.

About 250,000 Palestinians became refugees and moved into refugee camps in Lebanon, Jordan and other countries.

What did they want?

Israelis wanted to keep the land they had gained because the desert and mountains gave them safer borders. Arab countries and the United Nations wanted Israel to go back to its previous borders. Some Arab nations refused to recognize Israel as a legal country. To this day, arguments and discussions over borders and territories between the two sides continue.

TERRORISM

After the Six Day War in 1967, an organization called the Palestine Liberation Organization (PLO) began to speak for the Palestinians in the West Bank and refugee camps. Disagreements continued, but the Palestinians did not have an official army, tanks or aircraft. Instead they carried out **terrorist** attacks against Israeli soldiers and citizens. They **hijacked** aircraft and, for example, killed 11 Israeli athletes and coaches during the Olympic Games in 1972.

This graffiti in the West Bank town of Jericho shows a PLO fighter.

THIS IS WHERE I LIVE

Ramallah, West Bank

March 2013

Dear Jacob,

I am sorry I haven't replied sooner. My grandmother, who lives with us, couldn't decide whether she would ever talk to me again if I did, or ever talk to me if I didn't! She was so amazed to see the photo of your house because she used to live just two doors away from you!

We have had to get used to Israeli tanks driving along our streets.

Building on Palestinian land

Jewish settlers have been building homes on the West Bank and other Palestinian areas since the Six Day War in 1967. The United Nations says these **settlements** are illegal, but, despite this, the Israeli government allows the settlers to continue building.

This Israeli settlement is on Palestinian land

First she wept with happiness to see that her house is still standing, and then she wept because she can't live there now. She says I must write and ask you if the olive tree is still growing in the courtyard, and, if so, does it still produce a good crop of olives?

I live in a small flat in Ramallah with my four brothers and two sisters. Two of my brothers are older than me, and the others are all younger. We are very crowded. My parents would love to build a new house on the edge of Ramallah, but Israel doesn't allow Palestinians to live there because there is a Jewish settlement further up the hill.

I would like to hear how you live, and why your government makes us live like this.
Write again!

Sabra

WAR

13

Fighting about settlements

As well as expanding its borders, Israel has also increased its land by setting up Jewish-only communities on **occupied land**. This activity is illegal in international law, which states that an occupying power "shall not transfer parts of its own **civilian** population into the territory it occupies".

The United Nations, the United Kingdom and other countries have called on Israel to stop building.

More and more

Israelis began creating settlements in the West Bank, the Golan Heights and East Jerusalem after the Six Day War. There are more than 120 official settlements in the West Bank and they continue to get bigger.

Palestinian protests have not stopped the Israeli government from building more and more settlements.

Palestinians lose out

When land is cleared for a new settlement, the Palestinians living and farming there have to move out. Their homes are bulldozed and they lose their farms. Settlements are often built on the best farmland or over important sources of water, such as springs. Each Israeli settler, for example, uses around 280 litres (62 gallons) of water a day, while each Palestinian has access to around 80 litres (18 gallons) of water a day.

Many Palestinian families have been forced to leave land now occupied by Israel. Some live in refugee camps.

THE OTHER SIDE

About 547,000 settlers live in the West Bank, including about 197,000 people in East Jerusalem. Many are very religious **Haredi** Jews, who believe that God gave them the land. They say they have a right to it and will never give it up.

A SCARY WAY TO LIVE

Jerusalem, Israel
April 2013
Dear Salma,
    I've just spent the scariest weekend with my friend David He lives in a settlement overlooking Ramallah You can probably see it! We were having lunch, when we heard a lot of shouting and a Palestinian woman speaking through a **megaphone**.

Soldiers soon arrived to stop the protesters.

Murdered settlers

Some settlers have been murdered by Palestinian terrorists who have shot at them from passing cars. In June 2016, a 13-year-old girl was stabbed to death in the bedroom of her home in the West Bank Israeli settlement of Kiryat Arba.

A Palestinian olive grove.

My friend's parents told us to stay inside, so we went to the top of the house and looked out of the window.

A big crowd of Palestinians stood around the wall that surrounds the settlement. Some of them were younger than me! They were shouting that we had stolen their land. Then they threw stones over the wall until Israeli soldiers arrived and shot **rubber bullets** at them.

My friend David says that this happens a lot. He and his family have lived in their house for three years now. They farm the land in the settlement, and the Palestinians don't like that. One Palestinian man said that the settlers have stolen his olive grove, and now he has no way to make money.

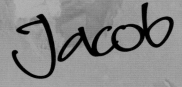

Jacob

CHAPTER TWO

LIVING WITH VIOLENCE

Most Palestinians and many Israelis live with the constant threat of violence. Palestinian children can be arrested and imprisoned for throwing stones or just for being near the scene of a protest or demonstration.

Unsafe at home

Israeli soldiers may force their way into Palestinian homes to arrest people or to take up a safe position when trouble breaks out. Sometimes, soldiers have forced families into one room and taken over the rest of the house for many days.

Palestinians in the West Bank have to live with Israeli soldiers watching them wherever they go.

HAMAS

The Palestinian organization Hamas is in charge of Gaza. Israel says it attacks Hamas because the group is determined to destroy Israel.

Drones and rockets

Israelis want to arrest or kill the Palestinians who are responsible for the terrorist attacks. If they suspect that a terrorist is in a particular house, they send an unmanned aircraft called a **drone** to bomb the house. Other people, including children, may be killed by mistake.

In return, Palestinians respond to Israeli action by attacking Israelis, particularly soldiers and settlers, and by firing rockets into Israeli villages near the border with Gaza.

Both Palestinian and Israeli homes have been destroyed by bombing.

WHAT CAN WE DO?

Ramallah, West Bank

May 2013

Dear Jacob,

I am sorry you were scared when you visited your friend in the settlement. Life is like that for us here pretty much every day.

Israel gets more than $3 billion (£23 billion) from the United States government every year, mostly for buying weapons. Israel has the most up-to-date weapons, aircraft, drones and **missiles**. We have just a few rockets that can hardly reach further than your borders.

Anyone who protests against the Israeli Army may be arrested and thrown into prison.

Palestinians in prison

Palestinians are under Israel law — but not the same law as Israelis. They are under Israeli **military law**. A Palestinian who throws a stone at an Israeli soldier can be sentenced to up to 20 years in prison. Between 2010 and 2015, around 1,200 Palestinian children were arrested each year by Israeli Army forces, most of them for throwing stones.

Palestinian youths throw stones in protest at the Israeli forces.

WAR

With no other weapons, Palestinians throw stones! My brother was arrested for throwing stones. He is now in prison in Israel, although he is only 15 His friend has just been released and says that the prisons are terrible.
I am scared for my brother. He won't be safe, even when he is released, because he can be arrested again at any time. In an Israeli court, it is his word against that of an Israeli soldier.

Salma

Suicide bombers

Palestinians have used more than stones to attack Israelis. Israel has also been attacked by **suicide bombers**, gunmen and rockets. The people who carry out these attacks are called terrorists by the Israelis and **martyrs** by the Palestinians.

Suicide bombers are people who strap explosives to their body and then travel to a target, such as an army post or shopping centre, to **detonate** the explosives. They know that they will kill themselves, but they hope that they will kill and injure Israelis, too.

Palestinians believe that their suicide bombings are justified, because they have suffered so many deaths at the hands of Israeli forces.

Palestinian bombers target ordinary Israelis, such as these people, as well as Israeli forces.

Rockets

Israelis who live near the border with Gaza are attacked by rockets and **mortars** fired from Gaza. Since the attacks began in 2001, more than 15,000 rockets and mortars have been launched, killing more than 30 people. At first, the rockets could reach no further than 16 kilometres (10 miles) inside the Israeli border. However, since Palestinian **armed groups** acquired more modern rockets, they have been able to hit towns and cities far into Israel.

MARTYRS

Palestinians say that people who kill themselves in order to attack Israelis are martyrs. They believe that suicide bombers attack the enemies of Islam and will go straight to paradise, or heaven. However, many Muslims say that the Koran forbids killing and that suicide bombers are **un-Islamic**.

MY COUSIN WAS KILLED

Jerusalem, Israel
June 2013
Dear Salma,
  I was shocked by your last letter, but we suffer violence too. My cousin was killed by a suicide bomber when I was only four years old.
  My cousin was travelling on a bus through part of Jerusalem where many Haredi (very religious Jews) live. The bus was crowded with Haredi children. A suicide bomber got on the bus, but no one realized it because he was dressed as a Haredi, too. When the bomber blew himself up, he killed 23 people. Seven of them were children like my cousin.

Like Palestinian children, Israeli children have also been victims of the conflict.

A separation wall is built

Israel began to build a **separation barrier** in 2002. It was planned to be around 700 kilometres (430 miles) long and is still incomplete, costing about £1.5 million per kilometre to build. However, it helped to reduce the number of suicide bombings from 55 in 2002 to 1 by 2007.

The separation barrier divides our countries.

WAR

Our family was so shocked and filled with grief to lose my cousin. We later learnt that the bomber was a terrorist from Hebron. It is not only buses that suicide bombers have targeted. They have blown themselves up in restaurants, shops and other crowded places.

There are fewer suicide bombers since Israel built the high security fence to separate the West Bank from Israel. It separates us, but it keeps us safer.

Yours,

Jacob

CHAPTER THREE

GOING NOWHERE

The Israeli government has certainly reduced the number of attacks on Israel, but this has come at a great cost to the Palestinians who live in the West Bank, East Jerusalem and Gaza.

Israel has set up hundreds of **checkpoints** and **roadblocks** in the West Bank. It has also built the separation barrier to control Palestinians getting into Israel. Only Palestinians with Jerusalem identity papers, a foreign passport or special permission from Israel can cross from the West Bank into Israel.

Palestinians often queue for hours to cross through the separation barrier into Israel.

Not easy to travel

Palestinians are not free to travel. Checkpoints and roadblocks make it very difficult to travel even a short distance inside the West Bank. Children are often delayed and questioned on their way to school by soldiers and settlers. There is no airport in Palestine, so to go abroad Palestinians must travel through one of Israel's three international airports. However, crossing into Israel first takes a long time.

Total control

Israel has control over everyone and everything that goes into or out of the West Bank and Gaza. This means that the Israeli authorities can quickly cut off supplies to Palestinians. They can also limit supplies, even of essential things such as medicines.

An Israeli official checks a passport. Soldiers can set up temporary checkpoints wherever they like.

FOR SAFETY'S SAKE

Israel says that it has to control the border so that Palestinian terrorists cannot sneak in and attack Israeli citizens and settlers. Sometimes the Israelis agree to reduce the number of checkpoints and roadblocks. However, when one checkpoint is removed, another one usually opens.

SUCH A LONG JOURNEY

Jericho, West Bank
July 2013
Dear Jacob,
I am writing from my cousin's house in Jericho. We are only 40 kilometres from Ramallah, but it took us two days to get here. We never know how long the journey will take. It could be four hours or four days.
It is almost impossible to drive because of the checkpoints and roadblocks. A roadblock is where Israelis block the road with dirt or concrete blocks, so you can walk, but not drive, through. We left our car at home and took taxis.

We used taxis like this one to get from one checkpoint to the next

Forbidden roads

The West Bank has hundreds of kilometres of new roads that Palestinians are not allowed to use because of the danger of terrorist attacks. The roads have been built for the settlers. Settlers speed along these roads, while Palestinians have to go far out of their way.

An Israeli soldier guarding a fast road through the West Bank

The first taxi dropped us at a checkpoint, where we waited for nearly two hours before the Israeli soldiers let us through. They thought my brother looked like a terrorist, so they questioned him and searched him for explosives.

We hired another taxi to take us to the next checkpoint. On the other side, we hired another taxi, and on it went. In the late afternoon, we stopped at my uncle's village and stayed the night with him. The next day, he drove us to Jericho. He took dirt tracks to avoid roadblocks, but it was such a long way round that we got to Jericho only in the afternoon.

Salma

WAR

Checkpoints

Israel controls all the checkpoints and border crossings into and out of the West Bank. The army is responsible for making sure that the crossings are secure so that no suicide bomber or terrorist crosses into Israel.

Getting through a checkpoint

Palestinians have to queue to cross a checkpoint. Soldiers call up each person one by one and check that they have the right papers. Palestinians often need special permission to travel from one place in the West Bank to another.

In 2015, there were 39 border checkpoints and 57 more within the West Bank. Soldiers also set up temporary checkpoints, called "flying checkpoints", so possible terrorists do not know where and when they will be stopped.

An Israeli soldier has stopped this driver to check what he is carrying in his car.

30

Ambulance – emergency!
It can take a long time for pedestrians to get through a checkpoint, but it takes even longer for a vehicle to be searched and checked. The Israelis say that people who are really ill or injured can pass through, but ambulances are searched first. Palestinians say it takes so long for ambulances to travel in the West Bank that many people, who could be saved, die on the way to hospital.

Israelis say that their tight border controls and checkpoints are justified because so many terrorist attacks have been made against Israeli soldiers.

BETWEEN THE BORDER AND THE WALL

The separation barrier does not follow the border that the United Nations established between Israel and Palestine. Instead, the barrier is built mainly on Palestinian land and takes in settlements near the border. Palestinians claim this is another way in which Israel is taking over their land.

IN THE ARMY

Jerusalem, Israel
August 2013
Dear Salma,
   It is so hot in Jerusalem now, but we are going on holiday next week to England to see family. It will definitely be cooler there! Ramallah must be as hot as Jerusalem, but I know you can't travel as easily as we can.

My friend has a sister in the Israeli Army. Most people have to serve in the Israeli Army when they are old enough.

Israeli Defence Forces

The military forces of Israel are called the Israeli Defence Forces (IDF). Most men do 2 years 8 months **military service** and women do 2 years. After military service, everyone becomes a member of the reserve force. They can be called back into military service for a month a year.

We are going now because my brother Nathan starts army training in September. My father is proud that his son will be an Israeli soldier. Nathan is proud, but my mother and I are scared. I know that everyone has to serve in the army to protect Israel, and I will do the same when I'm 18, but ...

There are so many "what ifs". If there is another war, he might be shot. He might have to fight in Gaza, Lebanon or Syria. Many soldiers on checkpoint duty have been injured or killed by Palestinian gunmen.

What if he arrests your brother? That would be awful. Or suppose he drives a tank or bulldozer into Ramallah. I wish we could all live in peace together.

Jacob

Smoke rises over the city of Gaza after it was hit by an Israeli bomb. The bombing raids continued every 20 minutes for 22 days.

Blockade of Gaza

In late 2008, Israel went to war against Gaza. After the war, Israel began a **blockade** of Gaza, allowing Palestinians to receive only limited supplies of food, water, fuel and electricity. Most ordinary goods were forbidden.

What happened?

In 2005, the Israeli leader, the prime minister, forced Israeli settlers to leave Gaza and withdrew the Israeli Army. Although the land was left for Palestinians alone to control, attacks on both sides continued. The number of rockets launched against Israel increased, and, on 27 December 2008, Israel bombed Gaza and invaded the area. The war lasted 22 days, killing 13 Israelis and more than 1,300 Palestinians. It devastated the people of Gaza.

The siege of Gaza

After the war, Palestinians could not rebuild their homes, schools or factories because Israel would not let them bring in building materials. The border between Gaza and Egypt was also closed, so Palestinians dug tunnels under it and smuggled in food and other goods, including weapons. Israelis bombed the tunnels, but then, in 2010, they allowed more items to be brought in. In 2011, the new government in Egypt also made it easier for some Palestinians to cross the border.

A mother mourns the death of her son during the Israeli bombing of Gaza. About 5,000 Palestinians, including many children, were also injured.

THE DAMAGE

During the Gaza war, about 6,500 Palestinian homes were completely destroyed or badly damaged. One million people in Gaza were left without electricity, and 500,000 people had no water. More than 1,000 factories and businesses were damaged, and thousands of people lost their jobs. Most Palestinians in Gaza now rely on **aid** for food.

TRAPPED IN GAZA

Ramallah, West Bank
September 2013
Dear Jacob,
    I have just received a letter from my cousin Maryam, who lives in Gaza. I thought we had it bad, but things are so much worse for her. She was happy because the Israeli government is allowing more things into Gaza, and now they can get chocolate, toys and ketchup. Good news for the children, but imagine being happy to have ketchup!

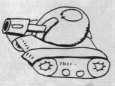

My cousin Maryam says they travel in a cart now. Imagine not being able to run a car!

Lifting the blockade?

The Israeli government bans anything it thinks can be used to make weapons or bombs, such as drills, **disinfectants** and fertilizers. In July 2010, Israel said it would lift the blockade in Gaza if and when Sergeant Gilad Shalit, an Israeli soldier captured by Hamas in 2006, was released. He was eventually set free in October 2011.

This Hamas fighter is holding a photo of Gilad Shalit, who was captured by Hamas.

The women can now buy washing machines, beds and other things, but they still have major problems. About 90 per cent of the water in Gaza is unhealthy to drink, but Israel won't let the people import disinfectant to clean it. They can have some building materials and tools but not drills and other items they need.

I so want to see Maryam again. I haven't seen her since 2010. Palestinians can't leave Gaza to go to Israel unless they are desperately ill, and it's not much easier getting into Egypt. She says there is so little fuel, her father has abandoned his car. They now use a donkey to pull a cart.

Why can't our politicians work this out?

Salma

WAR

37

CHAPTER FOUR

CAN WE LIVE TOGETHER?

There have been many attempts to help the Israelis and Palestinians to make peace. The United States, in particular, has arranged talks with both parties to reach a solution.

Oslo talks

In 1993, secret talks took place in Oslo, Norway, between the leaders of Israel and the PLO. They agreed to recognize each other's right to exist. They also agreed that the Israeli Army would gradually hand over control of the West Bank and Gaza to the Palestinians.

PEACE NOW

People hoped the Oslo talks would work, but neither Hamas nor the Israeli settlers accepted the deal.

Big problems

Most peace deals break down because they do not solve the main problems. Both sides in the Israeli-Palestinian disagreement want their own independent country where their people can live safely. However, the Israeli settlers in the West Bank remain a problem to this day.

The future of Jerusalem is also unsolved. Both sides want to have their capital in the ancient city. Israel took control of East Jerusalem during the Six Day War, and the number of Israelis living there has increased since then. They have knocked down many Palestinian buildings and taken the land for themselves.

Most Palestinians say that Israel must return to the borders they had before the Six Day War in 1967.

AN INDEPENDENT STATE

In 2011, the Palestinian National Authority, the organization that governs parts of the West Bank and Gaza, applied to become a member of the United Nations. The application was based on the borders between Israel and Palestine that existed before the 1967 war. The application was accepted by UNESCO, an organization within the United Nations, but it failed in the end, mainly because the United States **vetoed** it.

WE ARE NOT SO DIFFERENT

Jerusalem, Israel
October 2013
Dear Salma,
    I agree with you so much that the situation between Israelis and Palestinians must be worked out If the politicians can't do it, perhaps the people can! After all, we are not so different I was thinking about some of the many things that Jews and Muslims share.
    We both eat the same foods, and we even have similar rituals around some foods You can eat kosher food and we can eat some halal food
    Our religions have much in common. We believe in the same God, and we are all "children of Abraham". Our Hebrew Torah and your Koran share many stories and commands. We both pray several times a day, and we both have days when we fast
    We even have similar words for "peace". We say "shalom", and you say "salaam". Most of all, we already do things together here and in other parts of the world For example, in Spain my friend's sister plays in the West-Eastern Divan Orchestra.
    May peace come to both our peoples soon.
    In hope,

Jacob

A Middle Eastern orchestra

The West-Eastern Divan Orchestra was set up in 1999 by the Argentine-Israeli conductor Daniel Barenboim and his friend the Palestinian-American academic Edward Said. The members of the orchestra come from Israel, Palestine and other Middle Eastern countries. They have performed in many countries, including Israel and Palestine.

Here are two more similarities. We both place great importance on studying our holy texts and we both cover our heads.

Working together

Most Israelis and Palestinians want to live in peace, but very few of them have contact with each other or understand what life is like for "the other side". Several projects have been set up that bring Palestinians and Israeli Jews together.

Hand in Hand Arab-Jewish schools

Most Israeli and Palestinian children go to Jewish-only or Muslim-only schools. Hand in Hand schools are different. Half of the pupils are Jewish and half are Muslim. The lessons are taught in Hebrew and Arabic, and the two groups work together, make friends and learn to understand each other.

Further away than ever?

Hopes for peace continue, but a lasting resolution of the conflict seems further away than ever. In July 2014, Israel launched an attack on Gaza, which lasted for 50 days. It killed 2,139 Palestinians and 70 Israelis and destroyed 20,000 Palestinian homes.

All attempts at peace talks have failed, and Israel continues to expand the settlements in the West Bank and East Jerusalem.

This poster says, "Oasis of Peace" in English, Arabic and Hebrew. It shows the village (see box right) entwined with the dove of peace.

These children and teachers are at the school in Oasis of Peace. Here, Palestinian and Israeli children dress exactly the same.

OASIS OF PEACE

Wahat al-Salam-Neve Shalom is a village in Israel that means "Oasis of Peace" in Arabic and Hebrew. Israeli Jews and Israeli Palestinians have chosen to live together there for more than 40 years. They respect and understand each other and treat each other as equals. They educate their children together and work towards a peaceful solution.

A LONG WAY TO GO

Ramallah, West Bank
March 2016
Dear Jacob,
   It's been so long since I wrote to you,
you must have wondered why. We've had such
a difficult time here. My father was killed –
I can't bear to tell you about it – and it's
been so hard without him.
   But I found your letter again last week, and
I like what you said in it. The more that ordinary
people like you and I talk to each other, the
sooner we can find a solution.

Israeli protesters campaign for
peace beside the separation barrier.

PEACE NOW

Exchanging prisoners

In 2011, the Israeli soldier Gilad Shalit was released in exchange for 1,000 Palestinian prisoners. This seemed a hopeful sign, but the blockade on Gaza was not lifted and rockets continued to be fired from Gaza into southern Israel. In 2014, peace talks collapsed when Israel broke its promise to release 300 prisoners. Yet many people on both sides still hope for peace.

Perhaps if more Israelis can see how we live, a peaceful solution may be found

Last week, an Israeli organization called B'Tselem came to our street and handed out video cameras. They want us to film the problems in our everyday lives so that they can show the Israeli public how we live. They say that most Israelis have no idea.

Politicians are such fools! They make things worse because they only want to please their supporters, and they tell lies to justify themselves. Our friendship is a small beginning, and we have a long way to go.

Please keep writing!

Your friend,

GLOSSARY

aid help given to poor countries, usually by richer countries

armed group unofficial group of fighters

blockade something that stops people or goods from getting to or from a particular place

checkpoint place along a road where people and vehicles are stopped and their papers and baggage are checked

civilian not a member of the armed forces

detonate make a bomb explode

disinfectant liquid that kills germs

drone remote-controlled aircraft

Haredi very religious, Orthodox Jew

Hebrew language of the Israelis

hijack to seize control of a vehicle, such as an aircraft

martyr person who dies or suffers extreme pain for his or her religion

Mediterranean Sea sea that is situated between North Africa and Europe

megaphone device shaped like a funnel that makes a voice sound louder

military law law that is enforced by military organizations

military service period of time that some countries require people to spend training and serving in the army or other armed forces

missile flying bomb that is launched from land or sea

mortar shell fired by a type of cannon that is also called a mortar

Nazi party that ruled Germany during World War II

occupied land land that is controlled by another country following a military invasion

refugee person who is forced to leave home because of war or persecution

roadblock barrier in which obstacles are placed across the road to stop vehicles, and sometimes people, from travelling along the road

rubber bullet bullet made of hard rubber fired to scatter crowds of people without killing anyone

separation barrier high concrete wall and deep ditch built between Israel and the West Bank

settlement community of people – in Israel, one built on disputed land

suicide bomber person who wears explosives to kill or injure others and expects to die in the process

terrorist person who carries out violent acts against civilians to achieve a political goal

un-Islamic against Islamic teachings

United Nations international organization that includes representatives of most countries in the world, and which rules in cases of international disputes

veto action to override a vote that would make an agreement become law

FIND OUT MORE

Books

Israel (Countries Around the World), Claire Throp (Raintree, 2013)

Israel (Countries in the News), Michael Gallagher (Franklin Watts, 2006)

The Arab-Israeli Conflict (Timelines), Cath Senker (Franklin Watts, 2007)

The Middle East (Kingfisher Knowledge), Phil Steele (Kingfisher, 2006)

Websites

Discover more about why Israelis and Palestinians are fighting over Gaza:
www.bbc.co.uk/newsround/20436092

Find out more about controlled roads and checkpoints in the West Bank:
www.btselem.org/freedom_of_movement/checkpoints_and_forbidden_roads

Learn more about the Hand in Hand Jewish-Arab integrated schools:
www.handinhandk12.org

For maps of Jerusalem, Gaza, the West Bank and events in the Middle East conflict, see:
news.bbc.co.uk/1/shared/spl/hi/middle_east/03/v3_israel_palestinians/maps/html

See what life is like in the Arab-Israeli Oasis of Peace community:
wasns.org

INDEX